What CIOs Need To Know About Working With Partners

Techniques For CIOs To Use In Order To Be Able To Successfully Work With Partners

"Practical, proven techniques that will show you how to help your IT department become more effective by working with partners"

Dr. Jim Anderson

Published by:
Blue Elephant Consulting
Tampa, Florida

Copyright © 2013 by Dr. Jim Anderson

All rights reserved. No part of this book may be reproduced of transmitted in any form or by any means, electronic or mechanical, including photocopying, recording or by any information storage and retrieval system without written permission of the publisher, except for inclusion of brief quotations in a review.

Printed in the United States of America

Library of Congress Control Number: 2013923027

ISBN-13: 978-1494499976
ISBN-10: 1494499975

Warning – Disclaimer

The purpose of this book is to educate and entertain. This book does not promise or guarantee that anyone following the ideas, tips, suggestions, techniques or strategies will be successful. The author, publisher and distributor(s) shall have neither liability nor responsibility to anyone with respect to any loss or damage caused, or alleged to be caused, directly or indirectly by the information contained in this book.

Recent Books By The Author

Product Management

- Product Management Secrets: Techniques For Product Managers To Boost Product Sales And Increase Customer Satisfaction

- Customer Lessons For Product Managers: Techniques For Product Managers To Better Understand What Their Customers Really Want

Public Speaking

- How To Give A Great Presentation: Presentation techniques that will transform a speech into a memorable event

- How To Rehearse In Order To Give The Perfect Speech: How to effectively rehearse your next speech to that your message be remembered forever!

CIO Skills

- How CIOs Can Make Innovation Happen: Tips And Techniques For CIOs To Use In Order To Make Innovation Happen In Their IT Department

- CIO Communication Skills Secrets: Tips And Techniques For CIOs To Use In Order To Become Better Communicators

IT Manager Skills

- Secrets Of Effective Leadership For IT Managers: Tips And Techniques That IT Managers Can Use In Order To Develop Leadership Skills

- IT Manager Career Secrets: Tips And Techniques That IT Managers Can Use In Order To Have A Successful Career

Negotiating

- Learn The Skill Of Exploring In A Negotiation: How To Develop The Skill Of Exploring What Is Possible In A Negotiation In Order To Reach The Best Possible Deal

- Learn How To Argue In Your Next Negotiation: How To Develop The Skill Of Effective Arguing In A Negotiation In Order To Get The Best Possible Outcome

Miscellaneous

- Power Distribution Unit (PDU) Secrets: What Everyone Who Works In A Data Center Needs To Know!

- Making The Jump: How To Land Your Dream Job When You Get Out Of College!

Note: See a complete list of books by Dr. Jim Anderson at the back of this book.

Acknowledgements

Any book like this one is the result of years of real-world work experience. In my over 25 years of working for 7 different firms, I have met countless fantastic people and I've been mentored by some truly exceptional ones. Although I've probably forgotten some of the people who made me the person that I am today, here is my attempt to finally give them the recognition that they so truly deserve:

- Thomas P. Anderson
- Art Puett
- Bobbi Marshall
- Bob Boggs

Dr. Jim Anderson

This book is dedicated to my wife Lori. None of this would have been possible without her love and support.

Thanks for the best 21 years of my life (so far)...!

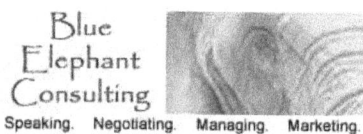
Speaking. Negotiating. Managing. Marketing.

Table Of Contents

SUCCESSFUL CIOS KNOW THAT THEY CAN'T DO IT ALONE 8

ABOUT THE AUTHOR 10

CHAPTER 1: IS CHANGE COMING TO IT IN THE FORM OF OUTSOURCING? 15

CHAPTER 2: IT INNOVATION TIPS FROM GM'S CIO 19

CHAPTER 3: 7 WRONG WAYS TO OUTSOURCE YOUR IT DEPARTMENT 22

CHAPTER 4: WHY DON'T IT ALLIANCES WORK OUT? 26

CHAPTER 5: SATYAM SCANDAL: CIOS NEED TO TALK WITH THEIR CFOS 29

CHAPTER 6: DEALING WITH VENDORS AFTER YOU'VE SIGNED THE DEAL 32

CHAPTER 7: PARTNER OR VENDOR: YOU MAKE THE CHOICE 37

CHAPTER 8: WHAT CIOS NEED TO KNOW ABOUT OFFSHORING 41

CHAPTER 9: MORE IT REGULATION: IS IT A GOOD THING FOR CIOS? 45

CHAPTER 10: IF AN IT PROJECT WASTES US$16B, IS IT THE CIO'S FAULT? 49

CHAPTER 11: 6 TIPS FOR PICKING THE RIGHT CLOUD PROVIDER TO PARTNER WITH 53

CHAPTER 12: 5 TIPS FOR CREATING EFFECTIVE BUSINESS PARTNERSHIPS 57

Successful CIOs Know That They Can't Do It Alone

In order to be a success, a CIO needs to be able to find and work with partners. These partners have to be committed to the same things that the CIO is: the overall success of his or her company and IT department.

However, finding the right partners can be quite a challenge. All too often alliances don't work out. CIOs need to take the time and study why some of these relationships are successful while others are not.

As difficult as it can be to find the right vendor, that is just the start of the relationship. CIOs have to understand that these types of relationships take care and maintenance. In order to get out of the relationship what you need, you are going to have to understand what the relationship is going to require over the long haul.

One of the most significant partnerships that most CIOs will become involved in have to do with the offshoring of IT assets. These are unique types of relationships and they come with their own special set of conditions and restrictions.

Just to make things more complicated, the arrival of cloud computing has created a whole new class of potential vendor partners for an IT department. Picking the right cloud provider is a brand new task for CIOs. We first have to understand the technology and then understand the firms that are providing it.

Finally, the importance of IT to every firm continues to grow. With this importance come additional responsibilities. The government has started to understand the impact that an IT department can have on the performance of a firm and so new legislation is being considered. CIOs need to both be aware of this and planning for it.

This book will provide CIOs with an overview of the different types of partners and relationships that they are going to need to develop. We'll explore offshoring, outsourcing, why alliances don't work out, and how to create effective business partnerships.

For more information on what it takes to be a great CIO, check out my blog, The Accidental Successful CIO, at:

www.TheAccidentalSuccessfulCIO.com

Good luck!

- Dr. Jim Anderson

About The Author

I must confess that I never set out to be a CIO. When I went to school, I studied Computer Science and thought that I'd get a nice job programming and that would be that. Well, at least part of that plan worked out!

My first job was working for Boeing on their F/A-18 fighter jet program. I spent my days programming fighter jet software in assembly language and I loved it. The U.S. government decided to save some money and went looking for other countries to sell this plane to. This put me into an unfamiliar role: I started to meet with foreign military officials and I ended up having to manage groups of engineers who were working on international projects.

Time moved on and so did I. I found myself working for Siemens, the big German telecommunications company. They were making phone switches and selling them to the seven U.S. phone companies. The problem was that the switches were too complicated. Customers couldn't tell the difference between one complicated phone switch from another complicated phone switch. Once again I found myself working with the sales and marketing teams to find ways to make the great technology that the engineers had developed understandable to both internal and external customers.

I've spent over 25 years working as an senior IT professional for both big companies and startups. This has given me an opportunity to learn what it takes to manage and IT department in ways that allow it to maximize its output while becoming a valuable part of the overall company.

I now live in Tampa Florida where I spend my time managing my consulting business, Blue Elephant Consulting, teaching college courses at the University of South Florida, and traveling to work with companies like yours to share the knowledge that I have about how to create and manage successful IT departments.

I'm always available to answer questions and I can be reached at:

Dr. Jim Anderson
Blue Elephant Consulting
Email: jim@BlueElephantConsulting.com
Facebook: http://goo.gl/1TVoK
Web: **www.BlueElephantConsulting.com**

"Unforgettable communication skills that will set your ideas free…"

Create IT Departments That Are Productive And A Valuable Asset To The Rest Of The Company !

Dr. Jim Anderson is available to provide training and coaching on the topics that are the most important to people who have to manage IT departments: how can I build a productive IT department (and keep it together) while at the same time providing the rest of the company with the IT services that they need?

Dr. Anderson believes that in order to both learn and remember what he says, speakers need to laugh. Each one of his speeches is full of fun and humor so that what he says "sticks" with everyone.

Dr. Anderson's CIO SkillsTraining Includes:

1. How to identify and attract the right type of IT workers to your IT department.
2. How to build relationships with the company's senior management in order to get the support that you need?
3. How to stay on top of changing technology and security issues so that you never get surprised?

Dr. Jim Anderson works with over 100 customers per year. To invite Dr. Anderson to work with you, contact him at:

Phone: 813-418-6970 or
Email: jim@BlueElephantConsulting.com

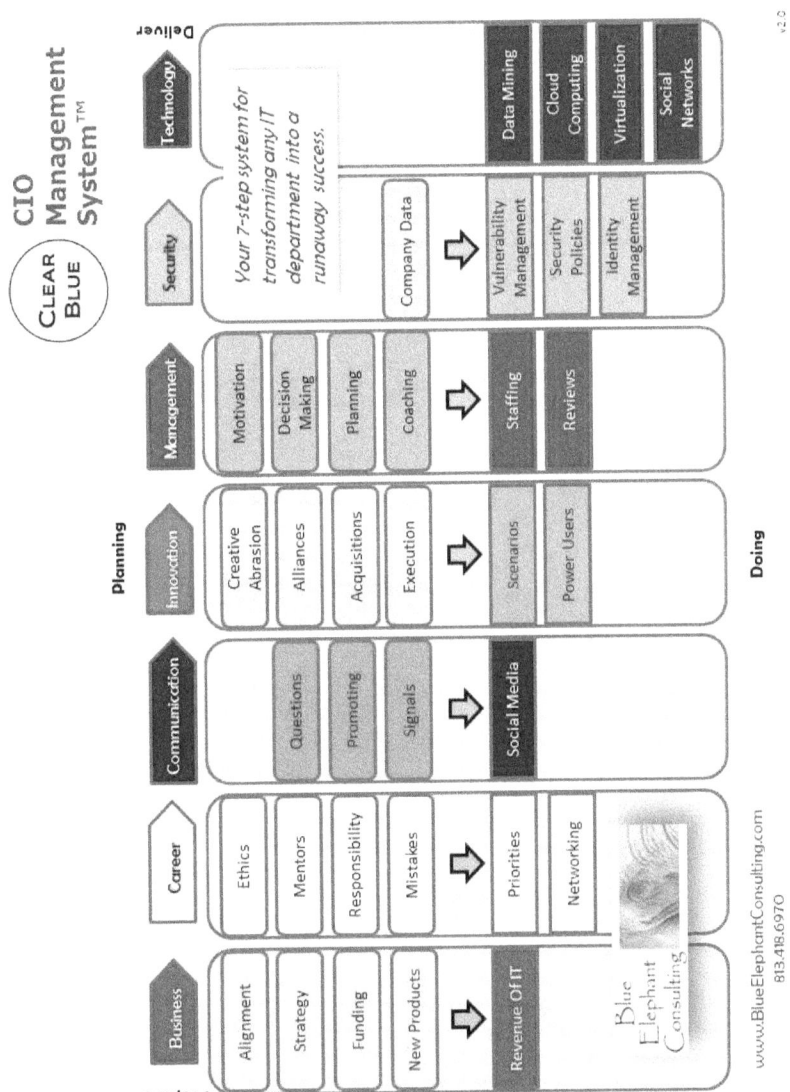

The **Clear Blue CIO Management System™** has been created to provide CIOs and senior IT managers with a clear roadmap for how to manage an IT department. This system shows CIOs what needs to be done and in what order to do it.

Chapter 1

Is Change Coming To IT In The Form Of Outsourcing?

Chapter 1: Is Change Coming To IT In The Form Of Outsourcing?

I just happened to run across an interesting article in Baseline magazine awhile back that pointed out a very interesting trend in IT that just might impact all of us. The good folks over at Royal Dutch Shell (the world's 3rd biggest oil company) have just announced a massive outsourcing deal with EDS/HP.

They appear to have gotten rid of just about all of their IT shop – lock, stock, and barrel. If they can outsource their entire IT shop, why can't your IT shop be outsourced completely also?

We like to talk about how to go about aligning IT with the rest of the business so that IT can play a strategic role in the company's success. Well, if you outsource all of IT that's not going to be happening any time soon!

Shell appears to have gotten rid of the parts of IT that have nothing to do with being an oil company. The following description of just exactly what is being outsourced comes from the press release about this deal:

> The activities in scope of outsourcing include designing, building, maintaining and operating the IT infrastructure, and cover the desktop and laptop computers, the telephone and handheld devices, the shared servers for running the applications that support business processes, the storage for data, and the networks and bandwidth for data and voice transmission.
>
> The infrastructure services enable Shell companies to use applications that support their business processes and goals, and enable staff and contractors for teamwork across the enterprise, whatever their

location, including offshore sites and some of the world's most remote areas.

What this means for folks in IT is that all of the day-to-day IT effort of keeping the network up and running has been outsourced. No need for DBAs, help desks, or Cisco certified folks anymore.

The Shell CIO, Alan Matula, has told the press that the real objective of the outsourcing deal was to allow the company to focus on its core business operations. Hmm, that does not sound like good news for those who work in any part of IT that can be considered to not be part of the "core"!

Although this is just one deal, it's being done by a multinational firm so the impacts won't be felt in just one country but rather in multiple countries. I think that this is a big deal. In effect, Shell said "enough is enough" to increasing IT costs that sure didn't seem to be providing any bottom line value back to the company. Oh oh, now that one big company has done this, what's to stop everyone else from doing the same thing?

I think that we are seeing the natural progression of outsourcing. Companies have now become so comfortable with what it means to outsource a function and the firms that they outsource the work to that they are willing to outsource any IT function that is not a part of what makes them competitive in their market.

There will always be a role for the part of IT that is developing the competitive tools that a firm needs to leap-frog its competition. Google's search engine, Ebay's auction platform, and Pixar's design tools will always be developed by in-house IT staff because they define the company. However, all the rest can probably be done better by someone else.

This means that CIOs are going to have to get better at managing outsourced operations because they are still responsible for the results. Additionally, IT managers are going to have to learn how to work with outsourcing shops in order to complete the projects that they have been given. It's a brave new world out there: get in, buckle up, and let's go!

Chapter 2

IT Innovation Tips From GM's CIO

Chapter 2: IT Innovation Tips From GM's CIO

The U.S. car manufactures have recently gone through some very, very rough times. Some had to declare bankruptcy, some had to be bailed out by the U.S. government, and so on. However, if you can put all of that aside for just a bit, then Ralph Szygenda who is the CIO at General Motors (GM) had a talk with the folks at eWeek and he has some suggestions on how IT departments can use outsourcing to drive innovation. Now there are two terms that you don't often see together! Let's see what this CIO has to tell us...

Who Does GM Outsource Their Work To?: About 60% of it goes to EDS (now part of HP) for historical reasons (GM once owned EDS), the rest goes to AT&T, HP. IBM, Capgemini, Covisint, and Wipro. Whew – is there anyone who is *not* on that list?

What Kind Of Money Are We Talking About Here?: In 2006 GM spent $7.5B on outsourcing contracts and they planned on spending another $7.5B in 2011.

How Many GM Employees Are Needed To Manage All This Outsourcing?: 1,500 GM employees manage the combined outsourcing vendors.

How Does GM Keep Their Outsourcing Vendors In Line?: GM continues to outsource additional business every year to the tune of 100's of millions of dollars. All of the outsourcing vendors want to win this additional business. GM uses a report card that gets updated every 6 months to let each vendor know exactly where they stand and then GM uses that report card to make decisions about who gets additional business.

Does GM Kick Out Under-Performing Vendors?: So far – no. However, all development of new systems are done at a firm, fixed price. That means that they start to lose money if they are missing a due date. There are some firms that have not been able to win new business because of how they have performed; however, nobody has been kicked off the team yet.

Are IT Costs Going Down Because Of This Outsourcing?: GM reports that they are spending a lot less on support and maintenance. However, they've taken these savings and are plowing them back into the development of new IT systems. The overall cost of operating the GM environment has been going down for the past 12 years and they are forecasting it to continue to do so for at least the next three years.

Why Did GM Decide To Outsource So Much Of Their IT Operations?: GM did not get into the business of outsourcing their IT operations to cut costs; however, the results have been that costs are being cut. The reason that GM originally decided to outsource their IT operations was because they had started with autonomous business units – every branch had its own IT shop. Over the course of 10 years they've gotten rid of over 5,000 systems. In 2006 they decided to consolidate their IT operations. Outsourcing IT operations has allowed processes to be standardized across the organization.

What Is The Key To GM's Innovation?: Szygenda says that it comes down to three things: standardization, simplification, and collaboration.

Chapter 3

7 Wrong Ways To Outsource Your IT Department

Chapter 3: 7 Wrong Ways To Outsource Your IT Department

Outsourcing, off-shoring, call it what you will, it's been with us long enough that you'd think that the rules for how to do it correctly would be well known, right? It turns out that this isn't always the case.

The current economy is probably going to have most IT shops looking for ways to further trim costs and, of course, outsourcing MORE will be an attractive option. Geraldine Fox and Nigel Hughes work over at Compass and they've got a few words of caution for the rest of us when it comes time to consider IT outsourcing.

It's all too easy to do this stuff the wrong way...

Skip The Planning, Dive Right In:

This is how all too many firms approach the outsourcing of their IT operations. All too often, firms view outsourcing as an opportunity to simply replace their expensive onshore headcount with less expensive offshore staff.

This view is not only short sighted, but just flat out wrong as lots and lots of firms discovered during the first wave of outsourcing in the 1990's. It takes time and lots of planning in order to move IT functions from inside the firm to an outsourcing shop. Once they are there, you're going to need more management resources than you have right now in order to stay on top of how the work is going.

"Lift & Shift":

Many firms attempt to just pick up their existing IT operations and move them over to the outsourcing operation hoping that lower salaries there will automatically deliver the savings that they are looking for. What's missing from this thinking is the simple fact that it will always take MORE people at the outsourcer to do the same job.

A good rule of thumb is to expect a 15% increase in headcount. Sure, you can probably move your ineffective IT operations offshore and experience some immediate short-term savings. However, very quickly these will vanish as outsourcing salaries continue to go up and staff turnover rates range annually from 25%-80%.

Out Of Sight, Out Of Mind:

Just dropping the work off and then not paying any attention to the people who are now doing the work is a clear recipe for disaster. Your firm is going to have to take on a whole new set of responsibilities.

These will include retaining outsource staff, investing in outsourced resources (training, orientation, retention), and making sure that they have a clear career path. Oh, and by the way, you had better be doing all of these things for your onshore / in-house staff or else they will become jealous very quickly!

More, More, More:

One well known reality of outsourcing is that that productivity will drop. This means that it's going to take more bodies to accomplish the same task. When you couple this with a high rate of turnover, you can pretty much wave goodbye to any outsourcing cost savings that you were counting on at least in the short term.

Smart firms realize that the solution to low productivity is not to throw more bodies at the problem; instead, you need to work with the outsourcer to fix the productivity problem at its source.

Everyone Else Is Not Doing Better At This Than You Are

No matter what your competition may be telling the press, don't worry. No firms are really seeing monster discounts because of their outsourcing efforts. Many firms claim that they are achieving 40% cost saving when the reality is that at best they really are seeing cost savings in the 20% range.

Hold Those Horses:

When you decide to outsource more of your IT operations, keep in mind that this will have a major impact on your firm. Companies don't do a good job of dealing with change and outsourcing part of your internal processes most definitely is change. Take some time to create the right mix of in-house and outsourced operations and then use a measured approach to implement it.

It Takes Two To Tango:

There is always the possibility that an outsourcing effort won't work out. If this happens, you need to realize that both your firm and the outsourcer are to blame.

Don't waste everyone's time pointing fingers at the outsourcer and expecting them to fix everything. Instead, acknowledge your part in creating the problem and then sit down with the outsourcer and get to work finding a way to fix it.

Chapter 4

Why Don't IT Alliances Work Out?

Chapter 4: Why Don't IT Alliances Work Out?

You would think that the more **alliances** that your company / IT department makes with other firms, then the better that they would become at making them. After all, practice makes perfect – doesn't it? It turns out that this is not always the case.

Koen Heimeriks has spent time studying **200 firms** that had formed more than 3,400 alliances. What he has found just might surprise you.

He found that those firms that had the most experience striking up alliances actually had **worse results** when compared to those firms who had moderate experience.

Why the difference? It turns out that there are two problems that develop in firms that already have a number of alliances:

1. they have a tendency to become **overconfident** in their alliance building skills, and

2. they can develop beliefs about alliances that are in actuality based on **unsupported ideas** about cause and effect.

So what can make an IT department's alliance with another firm actually work out well? It turns out that it's the **methods and procedures** that the firm uses to create alliances that will determine their eventual success. Established firms that already have many alliances will probably have **rigid** and inflexible business processes for making decisions and selecting partners.

However, IT departments with fewer existing alliances will have more **flexibility** built into their processes. An example of this would be where employees who have worked on previous alliances share information with the employees who are trying to create a new alliance. This type of discussion can lead to experimentation and allows novel approaches to each alliance opportunity.

So in the end, what does all of this lead to? Heimeriks reports that the larger firms who had many alliances and a more rigid alliance creation process had an alliance success rate of around **50%**. Those firms that had fewer alliances and a more flexible alliance creation process had an alliance success rate of around **71%**. Sure looks like flexible processes are the key to successful IT alliances!

Chapter 5

Satyam Scandal: CIOs Need To Talk With Their CFOs

Chapter 5: Satyam Scandal: CIOs Need To Talk With Their CFOs

Didn't we solve that whole outsourcing thing years ago? Specifically aren't the IT and the Finance departments on the same page when it comes to not only **IF** we should outsource some of the IT work, but also **HOW** it should be outsourced? If this is true, than what does the **Satyam scandal** mean for your IT / Finance relationship?

The Satyam Scandal

Just in case there is anyone out there who doesn't know what happened at Satyam, perhaps a quick review is in order. Satyam Computer Services is based in India, has a work force of **53,000** and operations in **66 countries**. They were very successful and served more than a third of the U.S. Fortune 500 companies.

Back in January the then CEO of Satyam, Ramalinga Raju, revealed that he and his CFO had been conducting a **massive fraud** – they significantly inflated the company's earnings and assets for years. Basically they had been losing money hand over foot. In January they revealed that 50.4 billion rupees, or $1.04 billion, of the 53.6 billion rupees in cash and bank loans the company listed as assets for its second quarter, which ended in September, were nonexistent. Poof!

Impact Of The Fraud

What this means for firms that do outsourcing business with Satyam is that the firm **might fold at any time** (perhaps you are one of these firms!) All of a sudden, outsourcing contracts that had appeared to be solid now seem to be not so solid. Most firms that outsource their work don't necessarily have a good

contingency plan for what to do if their outsourcing partner is suddenly unable to perform the work.

What Needs To Be Done

The Satyam scandal should serve as a **wake-up call** to CIOs everywhere. Outsourcing can never be done the same way that it's been done in the past. Here's what needs to change:

- **Finance Needs To Play A Role:** the IT department is responsible for making sure that the outsourcing company has the needed technical skills, but the Finance department needs to play a bigger role to make sure that the outsourcing firm can stay in business over time.

- **More Baskets For Your Eggs**: it's time to start to diversify your outsourcing activities in order to lower your risk profile. Detailed technical work needs to be moved around every so often so that not just one vendor knows how to do the work.

- **Update Your Contracts**: create shorter contracts that are more flexible. Make sure that you are not tied to a given outsourcer for too long just in case things start to go wrong – you might want to move your work to another outsourcer quickly.

Final Thoughts

India has now had their version of Enron / Worldcom. Hopefully it will serve as a **wakeup call** for all CIOs who outsource their work that greater due diligence needs to be done even as the world continues to move faster. By working more closely with Finance, CIOs can apply IT to enable the rest of the company to grow quicker, move faster, and do more.

Chapter 6

Dealing With Vendors AFTER You've Signed The Deal

Chapter 6: Dealing With Vendors AFTER You've Signed The Deal

When you become CIO, vendors will enter your life and they just won't leave. What this means is that they'll be a constant pain in your neck, always wanting your time and attention.

However, on the flip side, they will be a **valuable resource** that can provide you and your team with information and guidance that you couldn't get anywhere else. Don't do what too many new CIOs do and stop talking with vendors after the deal is signed...

What's In The Relationship For You

CIOs always have the same problem: they are being asked to do more and more with the same amount of resources and funding. The challenge is to do an **inventory** of what tools and talents you have available to you and then find ways to use those to perform the tasks that the company needs you to do.

One way to do this is to find new ways of using more fully the hardware, software, and services that the firm has already bought. As smart as your IT team is, there is **no way** that they can know all of the ins and outs of every IT tool that the department is currently using.

Ericka Chickowski over at CIO Insight points out that this is where your vendors come in. Assuming that you didn't burn your bridges with your vendors during the negotiation process, they can be **a fantastic resource** for you to draw on. Often new CIOs spend too much time looking only inside of the IT department and don't take the time to look outside in order to uncover this set of hidden resources.

How To Manage Your IT Vendors For Maximum Benefit

As your company's CIO, you will ultimately be responsible for controlling how your firm interacts with its IT vendors. You may not be part of every negotiation, but you certainly will end up **living with the results**. With that in mind, here are six things that you'll have to do as the CIO in order to get the most out of your IT vendor relationships:

1. **One Cook To Run The Kitchen:** those IT vendors are sly guys. They know that when they are dealing with inexperienced CIOs that they can always talk to other parts of the company if they don't like how things are going with the IT team. You need to step up and put your foot down both inside and outside of the company – let everyone know that you are the one who will ultimately be making the decision and nobody else. This will force your vendors to deal with you.

2. **Banish Confusion:** I can't tell you how many times I've seen this issue sink what could have been a great vendor relationship: when the IT department doesn't know what they really want. This is pretty simple right: if you don't know what you want, then there is no way that you're going to be able to tell the vendor what you want to buy. When this happens, the post deal relationship always seems to go poorly because nobody is happy – you're not happy with what you got and the vendor isn't happy because you're not happy.

3. **It's NOT All About Price:** I think that it's only the government that still sticks to the rule that they'll always buy from the lowest price vendor. Yes, the up-front price of whatever you are buying is important However, the cost of owning or using the product or

tool over the lifetime that your company will use it is what really counts. The CIO who can step back and determine what the true cost of a product is can make good negotiating decisions. Once again, choosing wisely will help you to have a good long-term relationship with your vendor.

4. **Boxing Yourself In:** One of the popular trends in IT these days is to reduce the number of suppliers that the firm is dealing with. This can have many benefits like being able to get greater discounts because you buy more from one supplier; however, there is also a dark side. You can easily get trapped into having to go along with what a vendor proposes if you've become too reliant on them. In order to have a healthy relationship with your vendor after the deal is struck, make sure that you keep your vendor options open.

5. **Forget The Little Guys:** Which vendors should you spend your time dealing with – the big guys or the little guys. We generally tend to favor the big guys, they do a slicker job. However, it's the smaller vendors who can more easily provide the customized services that you'll need as the CIO and they are the ones who will be willing to work more closely with your team after the deal is done.

6. **The Contract Is Just The Start:** CIOs who are just starting out often don't realize that after all of the effort that went into defining and signing the contract, the real work is only starting after everything has been signed. It's how you manage the day-to-day relationship with the vendor that you've selected that will really control how much value the company gets out of that contract.

What All Of This Means For You

All too often when new CIOs step into their position, they can get caught up in all of the **internal issues** that are always ongoing. However, if they do this, they may be missing one of the biggest "free" resources that they have available to them – their existing IT vendors.

The vendors know their products better than anyone else on the IT team and they have the experience with other IT departments in understanding how the tools can be used to solve real business problems. You'll need to be careful how you choose to deal with them, but they are **a great resource** in these cash strapped times.

Taking the time to realize that selecting a vendor and entering into a contract with them is **very much like a marriage** is what a new CIO needs to do. Sure the wedding is fun, but you need to realize that you are in it for the long haul and just like every other part of your CIO job, you're going to have to work at it in order to make it successful...

Chapter 7

Partner Or Vendor: You Make The Choice

Chapter 7: Partner Or Vendor: You Make The Choice

When you become CIO, you're going to be faced with the challenge of **picking your friends**. No, I'm not talking about being nice to the CEO and CFO – let's hope that they are already your friends. What I'm talking about is the collection of outside firms that provide your IT department with goods and services. They can't all be your best friend, so you've got some decisions to make...

The first thing that we should all agree on is that not all companies that you will be doing business with are created equal. What this means in practical terms is that the world is divided into two groups of businesses: **vendors and partners**.

A vendor is someone with whom you simply be doing business with. This is not to say that they aren't important, it's just that there's **not a lot of additional value** to be found in the relationship. A case in point might be the firm that supplies your IT department with paper: it's important, but it's not really a part of IT's long term strategy.

Things are different when you are working with a partner. In this case you are both always seeking a **win-win solution** because it's going to be a long-term relationship and it turns out that you are both in a position to help each other out.

Why Worry About What A Partner Is Thinking?

When you are the CIO, you're going to be busy. Worrying about your relationship with your partners is going to take some of your time. **Why bother?**

It turns out that it'll be worth the effort. The IT department's relationship with its partners is **a long-term investment**. This means that how you treat your partners today will end up being remembered for a very long time.

This is a relationship in which you always have to be thinking about what **the next step needs to be**. The key is to identify those steps that both companies can take together in order to add value to both firms.

It's when things go bad in the marketplace that the real value of having created a partnership with some of your suppliers will benefit your IT department. Taking the time to sit down and work with your partner in order to find ways that both of you can **remain whole during a market downturn** will end up benefiting both firms in the end.

How To Make Life Better For A Partner During A Downturn?

One of the secrets to being a successful CIO is **the ability to show creativity** when it comes to dealing with partners. During a rough patch, cash is probably going to be tight. You're going to have to come up with some innovative ideas if you are going to be able to help your IT department's partners out. Here are a few suggestions:

- **Add an extra year to a contract at a lower rate:** even though you may need to renegotiate a contract with your partner at a lower rate, help them out by extending the contract so that they know they have a guaranteed revenue stream.

- **Acting as a reference:** although your partner may not be able to get more cash out of you, by acting as a reference for them you may help them to close business with other companies that they couldn't get without your help.

- **Allow them to leverage your organization's brand:** something as simple as giving a partner permission to put your company's logo on their web site in order to identify who they do business with can be of great value to them.

- **Get a testimonial from you:** taking partner support to the next level, providing a partner with a testimonial that they can incorporate into their marketing material has a tangible value to them and will be appreciated.

What All Of This Means For You

In today's global economy, an IT department no longer consists of only your employees. Instead, it's **a spread out entity** that includes both internal staff as well as your partners.

By treating your partners well, you'll actually be able to expand the impact of your IT department. An added benefit of doing this will be that when **your partners come into contact with your customers**, they will do a good job of positively representing both your firm and your IT department.

Just in case you've missed the final reason that cultivating a select group of partners is worth your while, remember that **your CIO job may not last forever**. When your time as CIO is up at your current company, it sure would be nice to have a collection of firms in your industry that thought favorably of you...

Chapter 8

What CIOs Need To Know About Offshoring

Chapter 8: What CIOs Need To Know About Offshoring

Remember when using offshored resources as a part of an IT department was such a big deal? These days it's hard to find an IT department that doesn't have **at least some portion of its work done off shore**.

When you become CIO, offshoring is something that you're going to have to deal with. It turns out that things aren't as simple as they used to be…

When IT departments first started using offshoring there was really only one reason why they were doing it: **it provided staffing cost reductions of 40% or more**. It all seemed to be so easy: an IT department could move lots of low-value IT work to low-cost locations such as India and the Philippines. Let's be honest about this: outsourcing was really cost cutting by a different name.

When you become CIO you're going to be inheriting a different world. The favorite site of IT outsourcing has been India; however, India is changing.

One of the biggest changes is that salaries have been going up rapidly. In India, annual raises of 15% have become common.

On top of this, in the last year India has suffered from currency fluctuations, terrorist attacks, and financial fraud. When you become CIO you are going to have to be **looking beyond India** for locations to house your outsourcing.

The New World Of Outsourcing

You're going to have to do some serious thinking when it comes time to determine how best to use outsourcing with your IT department. Just before the recent global recession the #1 reason that IT departments were using offshored resources was **to accomplish cost cutting objectives**.

The impact of the recent global recession is going to be your friend when it comes to offshoring. Over at the consulting firm Gartner, they are predicting that outsourcing prices **will drop an average of 10%**. However, as CIO you are going to need to be careful here.

It turns out that agreeing to specific IT cost cutting goals isn't the hard part, maintaining them is. What many IT departments have discovered is that low hourly rates won't save much money if the **total hours needed** to accomplish a given task are higher than you estimate.

Another issue for a CIO to consider will be **how long your contract with the offshoring firm should last for**. The first generation of outsourcing contacts tended to be last for lengthy time periods: 10 years was common.

This was being done in order to "lock-in" the cost savings. However, the need to have the ability to adjust to changing market conditions has changed this – CIOs now want shorter-term contracts.

Of course, nothing is ever that simple. It turns out that for certain IT professional services that require a **higher percentage of highly skilled workers**, the offshore staffing providers will insist on longer-term contacts. The reason for this is because the suppliers say that they can't attract the workers that they need unless you are willing to sign contracts that cover longer time periods.

On the positive side, although with a bit more complexity, you will now have **more options for where you can do your offshore work**. Some of the most popular outsourcing destinations in a recent survey of firms that were considering it included: United States (22%), China (16%), India (13%). Also on their list were the Philippines, Mexico, Costa Rica, and Jamaica.

What All Of This Means For You

When you become CIO, **you will be offshoring some of your IT work**. What used to be a relatively simple decision to send some of your low-value IT grunt work over to India has become much more complicated.

India is still an attractive destination for a number of reasons. However, it has **become less attractive than it once was** and a number of competitive alternatives have now shown up.

It will take time and effort on your part in order to **properly evaluate your options** and decide what is correct for your IT department. You can't go wrong with the decision to offshore some of your IT workload, it's just making the right decisions on where the do the work that will require all of your CIO skills…

Chapter 9

More IT Regulation: Is It A Good Thing For CIOs?

Chapter 9: More IT Regulation: Is It A Good Thing For CIOs?

Software is all around us. CIOs depend on it to keep the company up and running.

If for some reason, a company's critical applications stop running, run incorrectly, or divulge private data to bad guys, there's a good chance that **the company is going to quickly have a new CIO**. If only there was some way to make software more reliable so that CIO's could spend their time focusing on the things that really matter…

3 Possible Futures For Software

You would think that CIOs would have already used their collective influence to get software vendors to **do the right thing**. However, as system outages that still exist today clearly show – this has not happened.

Thomas Smedinghoff is a lawyer who studies science and technology law. According to Smedinghoff, there are three possible futures for how software vendors are going to be required to do a better job of supporting CIOs:

1. Increased legal obligations for software vendors to do a better job of ensuring that their applications and associated communications are secure.

2. A much bigger responsibility to tell the world when there is a security breach.

3. Defining just what is meant by "reasonable security" and then ensuring that every application provides at least this level of protection.

What's Coming Down The Road

This of course leads a CIO to the next question: **which one of these future possibilities is going to happen (or will it be all of them?)** Smedinghoff points out that little by little, the responsibility to disclose when a personal data breach occurs is getting written into laws in each state.

Legal scholars are predicting that within the next 10 years or so CIOs should expect that their IT vendors will be **required by law** to improve both the security as well as the quality of their software applications. Toyota's recent car troubles may end up representing a first step in this direction.

Where does all of this lead to? Once again those legal scholars are predicting that by 2015 we should expect software vendors to find themselves being required to clearly specify their products capabilities as well as their limitations. What will give these words some bite is that they will have had to be verified by 3rd party certification firms.

What All Of This Means For You

When you become CIO, running an IT department will be much different than it is today. While that is **good news**, it also means that you're going to have a different set of tasks that you're going to have to do.

Gone will be the days in which you had to spend so much time and energy **just keeping applications up and running not to mention secure**. Now you'll be spending a lot more time during the selection process doing double checks to make sure that each vendor's product truly has been verified and certified by reputable 3rd party firms.

Yes, your life as a CIO will have become **much more**

manageable because you should experience fewer fire drills. However, you had better start getting ready to become a good fact checker so that you choose the right vendor after all the rules have been changed...

Chapter 10

If An IT Project Wastes US$16B, Is It The CIO's Fault?

Chapter 10: If An IT Project Wastes US$16B, Is It The CIO's Fault?

It seems like a classic IT problem. You've got a lot of separate medical facilities all trying to provide medical services to people who live in the same country. What's even better is that everyone is taking part in a nationally provided health care program.

It sure seems like **creating a single database to hold everyone's healthcare records** would be an almost no-brainer. Over in the U.K. they tried to do this, and things have not gone as they were planned.

The Problem With Lorenzo

In the U.K. the National Health Service (NHS) is the branch of the government that is responsible for providing health care to British citizens. As you might well imagine, the amount of data associated with this task is huge. Back in 2002 a decision was made to **create a single unified database system that would store customer information**. Sounds like a typical IT project doesn't it?

The new NHS computer system was to be called Lorenzo. This IT system was supposed to store data for 220 trusts in the north, eastern England and the Midlands at a cost of £3.1bn (US$4.96B). As is the case in far too many IT projects, things didn't go well. Now the final contract for that project alone **is likely to cost the Department of Health £2.2bn (US$3.52B)** and cover only 22 trusts.

This project is being called the biggest IT failure ever seen. The causes of the problem are many and a lot of different people contributed to them. However, it is believed that the NHS's particular problems stem from the original contracts signed before 2002. When there's an IT failure of this size, the question has to be asked: **where was the CIO while all of this was going on?**

What The CIO Should Have Done

So who is the CIO of the NHS? It turns out that **the CIO position has been a bit of a revolving door.** Christine Connelly held the CIO job from 2008 – 2011. Katie Davis then held the position from 2011 – 2012. Christopher Rieder now holds the position. It can be hard to tell who's in charge when the players keep changing!

So what did the CIO not do here? The Lorenzo project was launched in 2002 but was beset by changing specifications, technical challenges and disputes with suppliers **which left it years behind schedule and over budget**. In September 2011 ministers announced they would dismantle the National Programme but in an effort to salvage something from the failure said they would keep the component parts in place with separate management and accountability structures.

This attempt to get something out of the program ended up not working. The new structures have been examined and **a number of significant failures have been found**. The end result, is that very little of a very expensive project is going to produce any real value.

So what did the CIO fail to do? Ultimately, the negotiation of the contract with the IT vendors was the responsibility of the CIO. **The CIO should have renegotiated its original £3.1bn contract** with the IT systems group Computer Science Corporation for care records systems across 220 trusts in the North, Midlands and East, following delays and problems.

However, this never happened. As of today, CSC has still not delivered the software and "not a single trust has a fully functioning Lorenzo care records system". CSC's contracts could not be cancelled because a legal challenge by the company may well have succeeded. The CIO did not play a significant role in setting up these IT contracts and **that's why things got so far out of hand**.

What All Of This Means For You

The Brits have a real problem on their hands. They've spent a lot of money to create what should be a fairly straightforward IT database system of the people who are using their national healthcare system. However, after having spent US$16B, **they still don't have a working system**. Is the CIO to blame?

What went wrong here? It appears as though this is a pretty simple case of the IT arm of the British government **entering into some poorly worded long-term contracts**. The contracts seem to have not spelled out how changes were going to be handled and somehow let the vendors get off the hook without having to deliver a working solution. The CIO is ultimately responsible for every contract that the IT department signs, so yes – this is the CIO's fault.

What should have happened is that **professional contract negotiators should have been brought in to handle the creation of the IT contracts**. People who do this for a living would have never signed the contracts as they stand today. A CIO always needs to know when to reach outside for assistance.

Chapter 11

6 Tips For Picking The Right Cloud Provider To Partner With

Chapter 11: 6 Tips For Picking The Right Cloud Provider To Partner With

Face it, we are all going to **move our company's IT applications into the cloud eventually**. Just exactly where that cloud is going to be located and who will be running it for us is another question. What questions does a CIO need to ask when you are trying to select the right cloud vendor for your company?

5 Questions To Ask A Cloud Vendor

You wouldn't buy a car without doing your homework and asking the car dealer a bunch of questions, right? The same thinking should go into how you go about selecting a cloud provider for your company's valuable IT applications. The trick is to **know what questions you need to be asking**. Here are 6 of the most critical questions that you are going to need to get answers to:

1. **Experience:** You really don't want your company's applications to be the first ones that go into this vendor's cloud. You would prefer that they have done this many time before. Any company can look good in their marketing brochures, but the real proof will be when they can show you a list of their current customers. Look for proof of awards and anecdotes from known industry sources. Ask around: do you know anyone else who has gone with this vendor and what has their experience been like?

2. **Try Before You Buy:** Signing up with any cloud provider is a big risk for anyone who has the CIO job. If you've made a mistake, you'll know right off the bat. Make sure that you always have an "out". Make sure that you can pilot your solution with them before you get locked

into a long-term contract.

3. **Price Protection:** If there is one thing that we all hate, it's buying something and then discovering that we could have gotten it cheaper if we had only waited a bit. When you are negotiating the terms of your contact with your cloud provider partner, make sure that you build price protection into your contract. If they drop their prices while your contract in in effect, you should be able to take advantage of their best prices and not be locked in to the prices that were in effect when you signed the contract.

4. **It's All About The SLA:** Serviced Level Agreements (SLAs) are how you'll measure the level of service that your cloud provider is delivering to you. You'll want to create a custom SLA that meets your company's specific needs; however, at a bare minimum it's going to have to deal with issues such as availability, transaction time, storage, and performance. Make sure that you spell out what the cloud provider is going to have to do if they can't keep up their end of the SLA.

5. **Transparency:** Once you move your applications into the cloud, you will undoubtedly run into some problems. The big question is going to be where are those problems coming from: your applications or the cloud that they are running in? If you can't peer "into" the cloud, you'll have a tough time answering this question. You need to insist on having some level of transparency into the cloud so that you can check on things like monitoring and operational management, performance management, and change management,

6. **Bad Things Happen, Are They Ready?:** In this world that we live in, bad things do happen: freak storms, power outages, etc. Your cloud provider will experience these

types of things – will they be ready for them? You should insist on seeing their disaster recovery plan. Review it with them and see if you get a sense that they are really ready or is it just a sheet of paper that they hope to never have to use?

What Does All Of This Mean For You?

The arrival of the cloud is poised to change how the person in the CIO job runs their IT department. Eventually, **some or all of the company's applications will be moved to the cloud**. In order to ensure that they continue to operate reliably, CIOs need to know what questions they need to ask cloud vendors before making a selection.

Asking the right questions will ensure that you get the right cloud provider for your company. Make sure that they've done this before, that they offer a trial period, and that there is price protection built into the contract that they offer. SLAs are critical as well as your ability to peer into their operations. Finally, planning for the worst is a necessity so make sure that there is a disaster recovery plan in place.

Some of these questions may seem rather basic, but they are all critical. When it comes to something new and shiny like "the cloud" it can be all too easy to **forget to ask the really important questions**. Take the time to ask the right questions and you'll be sure to end up with the right cloud partner for you.

Chapter 12

5 Tips For Creating Effective Business Partnerships

Chapter 12: 5 Tips For Creating Effective Business Partnerships

As the CIO you are faced with a double challenge: despite the importance of information technology you have a limited budget and you have limited resources. This means that in order to get everything done that the rest of the company is expecting you to do, you are going to have to get creative. One way to do this is to get some outside help in the form of partnering with other businesses. The secret to success lies in knowing how to do this.

5 Tips For Establishing Business Partnerships

One of your jobs as CIO is to always be on the lookout for partners who can help your IT department achieve more. The difference between a partner and a vendor is that a partner won't be trying to sell you anything. Rather, they will be **trying to grow their business by working with you**. In order to determine if a given company would be a good partner, here are 5 tips for evaluating their potential:

1. **Inside Your Industry Is Where The Best Potential Partners Are:** Studies have shown that when a CIO chooses to partner with a company that is within his or her industry, this produces the best results. The thinking is that your IT department will be able to provide something that they can't and vice versa.

   Their hope is that by partnering with your IT department, they will develop new skills or insights that they can then use to bring in new customers. A good way to find potential partners is to check out their web sites and see if they have a "partners" page. If they are already partnering with other companies in your industry, then they may be a good candidate for you to partner with.

2. **Make The Effort – Reach Out:** No matter how long you've been a CIO, this is the scary part. The company that you are thinking about partnering with probably doesn't know about you. You are going to have to take the initiative. Find a way to get in contact with them. Reaching out through a common friend is the best way, but you can always use their web site or even LinkedIn to make contact.

3. **Create A (Simple) Plan:** If the other company expresses interest in partnering with you, then you are going to need to show up with a plan for how you can work together. Your plan needs to clearly show how the partnership is going to benefit both of you.

    Keep it nice and simple – there is no need to complicate things at this early stage of the game. A good way to get things started is for both firms to cross-promote each other's offerings. Give that a try and see where things go from there.

4. **Test, Test, Test:** You can never know if a partnership is going to work out from the start. This means that you are always going to have to be testing the partnership in order to make sure that both of you are getting out of it what you need. Ultimately, it's going to come down to what your IT department's customers think – with the partnership in place have you become more valuable to them?

5. **Dance With Other Partners:** No one partner is going to be able to provide your IT department with all of the extra resources that you are going to need. Even while you work with your new partner, you are going to want to still be exploring partnering with other firms. It is

entirely possible that you may bring on board additional partners that your existing partners will also be able to work with.

What All Of This Means For You

The CIO is always dealing with limitations on what they can do: limited budgets, limited staff, and, of course, limited time. One creative way that they can overcome these limitations is to **partner with other businesses** in order to be able to accomplish more of what the rest of the business is expecting them to do.

In order to set up an effective business partnership, a CIO has to be able to find other businesses within his or her own industry – **similarities can help to make a partnership work out**. The next step is to overcome any doubts that you might have and reach out. Every partnership is a test. Give it a try and see if it works. If it doesn't, then try different partners.

The good news for CIOs is that there is a virtually unlimited number of firms that may be suitable partners for them. The trick will be determining which ones hold the **highest probability of being good partners**. Take the time to follow these 5 tips and you just might find that with your new partners you are a CIO who can do more with what you have.

It's from the forge of failure that the steel of success is formed.

Hard Work Does Not Guarantee Success, But Success Does Not Happen Without Hard Work.

- Dr. Jim Anderson

Create IT Departments That Are Productive And A Valuable Asset To The Rest Of The Company !

Dr. Jim Anderson is available to provide training and coaching on the topics that are the most important to people who have to manage IT departments: how can I build a productive IT department (and keep it together) while at the same time providing the rest of the company with the IT services that they need?

Dr. Anderson believes that in order to both learn and remember what he says, speakers need to laugh. Each one of his speeches is full of fun and humor so that what he says "sticks" with everyone.

Dr. Anderson's CIO Skills Training Includes:

4. How to identify and attract the right type of IT workers to your IT department.
5. How to build relationships with the company's senior management in order to get the support that you need?
6. How to stay on top of changing technology and security issues so that you never get surprised?

Dr. Jim Anderson works with over 100 customers per year. To invite Dr. Anderson to work with you, contact him at:

Phone: 813-418-6970 or
Email: jim@BlueElephantConsulting.com

Photo Credits:

Cover - By: John
http://www.flickr.com/photos/mtsofan/

Chapter 1 - By: Paul Keller
http://www.flickr.com/photos/paulk/

Chapter 2 - By: jm3 on Flickr
http://www.flickr.com/photos/jm3/

Chapter 3 - By: Vitor Lima
http://www.flickr.com/photos/vitorcastillo/

Chapter 4 - By: Jennie Ivins
http://www.flickr.com/photos/autumn2may/

Chapter 5 - By: Mark Hillary
http://www.flickr.com/photos/markhillary/

Chapter 6 - By: anyoccasioncakes
http://www.flickr.com/photos/anyoccasioncakes/

Chapter 7 - By: Marco Abis
http://www.flickr.com/photos/matley0/

Chapter 8 - By: ILO in Asia and the Pacific
http://www.flickr.com/photos/iloasiapacific/

Chapter 9 - By: James Manners
http://www.flickr.com/photos/jmanners/

Chapter 10 - By: Ray Forster
http://www.flickr.com/photos/94418464@N08/

Chapter 11 - By: Sam Howzit
http://www.flickr.com/photos/aloha75/

Chapter 12 - By: thetaxhaven
http://www.flickr.com/photos/83532250@N06/

Other Books By The Author

Product Management

- Product Management Secrets: Techniques For Product Managers To Boost Product Sales And Increase Customer Satisfaction

- Product Development Lessons For Product Managers: How Product Managers Can Create Successful Products

- Customer Lessons For Product Managers: Techniques For Product Managers To Better Understand What Their Customers Really Want

- Product Failure Lessons For Product Managers: Examples Of Products That Have Failed For Product Managers To Learn From

- Communication Skills For Product Managers: The Communication Skills That Product Managers Need To Know How To Use In Order To Have A Successful Product

- How To Have A Successful Product Manager Career: The Things That You Need To Be Doing TODAY In Order To Have A Successful Product Manager Career

- Product Manager Product Success: How to keep your product on track and make it become a success

Public Speaking

- How To Give A Great Presentation: Presentation techniques that will transform a speech into a memorable event

- How To Rehearse In Order To Give The Perfect Speech: How to effectively rehearse your next speech to that your message be remembered forever!

- Secrets To Creating The Perfect Speech: How to create a speech that will make your message be remembered forever!

- Secrets To Organizing The Perfect Speech: How to organize the best speech of your life!

- Secrets To Planning The Perfect Speech: How to plan to give the best speech of your life

- How To Show What You Mean During A Presentation: How to use visual techniques to transform a speech into a memorable event

CIO Skills

- Critical CIO Management Skills: Decision Making Skills That Every CIO Needs To Have In Order To Be Able To Make The Right Choices

- How CIOs Can Make Innovation Happen: Tips And Techniques For CIOs To Use In Order To Make Innovation Happen In Their IT Department

- CIO Communication Skills Secrets: Tips And Techniques For CIOs To Use In Order To Become Better Communicators

- Managing Your CIO Career: Steps That CIOs Have To Take In Order To Have A Long And Successful Career

- CIO Business Skills: How CIOs can work effectively with the rest of the company!

IT Manager Skills

- Staffing Skills IT Managers Must Have: Tips And Techniques That IT Managers Can Use In Order To Correctly Staff Their Teams

- Secrets Of Effective Leadership For IT Managers: Tips And Techniques That IT Managers Can Use In Order To Develop Leadership Skills

- IT Manager Career Secrets: Tips And Techniques That IT Managers Can Use In Order To Have A Successful Career

- IT Manager Budgeting Skills: How IT Managers Can Request, Manage, Use, And Track Their Funding

Negotiating

- Learn The Skill Of Exploring In A Negotiation: How To Develop The Skill Of Exploring What Is Possible In A Negotiation In Order To Reach The Best Possible Deal

- Learn How To Argue In Your Next Negotiation: How To Develop The Skill Of Effective Arguing In A Negotiation In Order To Get The Best Possible Outcome

- How To Open Your Next Negotiation: How To Start A Negotiation In Order To Get The Best Possible Outcome

- Preparing For Your Next Negotiation: What You Need To Do BEFORE A Negotiation Starts In Order To Get The Best Possible Deal

Miscellaneous

- Power Distribution Unit (PDU) Secrets: What Everyone Who Works In A Data Center Needs To Know!

- Making The Jump: How To Land Your Dream Job When You Get Out Of College!

Techniques For CIOs To Use In Order To Be Able To Successfully Work With Partners

> This book has been written with one goal in mind – to show you how you work with partners. There's too much for a CIO to accomplish by themselves. Selecting and working with the right partners is the key to making your IT department a valuable asset to your company!
>
> **Let's Make Your CIO Career A Success!**

<u>What You'll Find Inside:</u>

- **7 WRONG WAYS TO OUTSOURCE YOUR IT DEPARTMENT**

- **WHY DON'T IT ALLIANCES WORK OUT?**

- **DEALING WITH VENDORS AFTER YOU'VE SIGNED THE DEAL**

- **6 TIPS FOR PICKING THE RIGHT CLOUD PROVIDER TO PARTNER WITH**

Dr. Jim Anderson brings his 25 years of real-world experience to this book. He's been a senior IT executive at some of the world's largest firms. He's going to show you what you need to do (and not do!) in order to make your CIO career a success!

www.ingramcontent.com/pod-product-compliance
Lightning Source LLC
Chambersburg PA
CBHW071807170526
45167CB00003B/1213